ARMOUR OF GOD

A practical and creative study

OLIVIA AMARTEY AND
MARTHA SHRIMPTON

First published in Great Britain in 2024

Essential Christian, 14 Horsted Square, Uckfield, TN22 1QG Tel: 01825 746530
Email: info@essentialchristian.org Web: essentialchristian.org
Registered charity number 1126997

SPCK, SPCK Group, Studio 101, The Record Hall, 16–16A Baldwin's Gardens, London, EC1N 7RJ
www.spckpublishing.co.uk

SPCK does not necessarily endorse the individual views contained in its publications.

British Library Cataloguing-in-Publication Data
A catalogue record for this book is available from the British Library

Paperback ISBN: 978-0-281-09045-7
Ebook ISBN: 978-0-281-09046-4
Audio ISBN: 978-0-281-09047-1

1 3 5 7 9 10 8 6 4 2

Typeset by Mark Steel, mark@marksteel.co

First printed in Great Britain by Clays Ltd, Bungay, Suffolk, NR35 1ED
Ebook by Fakenham Prepress Solutions, Fakenham, Norfolk NR21 8NL
Produced on paper from sustainable sources

Contents

Introduction *Words from Olivia Amartey*

The world of Marvel has seen a resurgence over the last decade. What is it about heroes and anti-heroes that continues to fascinate us? Perhaps it's their unique superpowers, be it invisibility, elasticity or super-strength, which enable them to take on evil and win. Or perhaps it's because they are the guardians of a superior knowledge that sets them apart from their fellow human beings even while they operate within the mundane and familiar.

Paul's letter to the Ephesians deals with topics that lie at the very core of what it means to be a Christian. It is a book of two halves: one concerns our position in Christ (chapters 1–3) and the second focuses on our practice on earth (chapters 4–6). From the beginning to the end, Paul comprehensively outlines what it means to be chosen and made alive in Christ; to live purposefully and in unity in the body of Christ. The letter ends with Paul outlining a practical application of just how to do this, and he does so by drawing on the flesh-and-blood superheroes of his day: the Roman army.

The Roman army: a formidable fighting force

The Roman army was the largest fighting force in the ancient world. Its unequalled discipline, strict training and superior weaponry enabled it to become the greatest military force in world history. A Roman soldier's armour was instrumental to his fighting prowess and – aligned with comprehensive knowledge of the enemy, the ability to swiftly deploy countertactics and excellent organisation – was the reason for the army's success. They were so good that they often took on other armies ten times bigger and won!

The armour of God is our super-suit! Throughout millennia, Christians just like you and me have taken Paul's advice, donned God's armour, fought the good fight of faith and won their unique battle.

Thy kingdom come... deliver us from the evil one

It is all too easy for us as modern-day Christians to believe that we are sophisticated, cultured and switched-on believers, especially when compared to first-century Christians. For some of us, the mention of Satan at best conjures up a shadowy supernatural being and is the stuff of childhood fables. In this day of Facebook, TikTok and Insta, such a belief may lead to ridicule and derision – so it's best to keep quiet about him, whoever he is.

Many of us are acquainted with the Lord's Prayer. Through it, Jesus has provided the disciples (and us) with the perfect model by which to frame our prayers. But two-thirds of the way down we read 'deliver us from evil', and we see that Jesus is not just addressing evil; he is indirectly pointing us to the originator and instigator of that evil, Satan himself.

We may well have read Gospel narrations of Jesus' encounter with the devil. But how are we to interpret and relate those to our lives today? It is well beyond the scope of this workbook to exposit on evil, its origin and its embodiment. However, if Jesus talks about the devil or the evil one, we would be wise to take heed. Paul also tackles this subject head-on. Here, as he concludes his message to the Ephesians, he comprehensively explains how Christians are to frame and develop their ability to both stand and withstand (Ephesians 6:13).

Struck by the uniform of the Roman soldiers guarding him as he writes from prison, he weaves this imagery into the narrative of his letter to the Ephesians.

Your personal training programme

Everything is preparation; preparation is everything

What a wonderful play on words. This phrase outlines a fundamental truth of life: that success in achieving a goal is a mix of anticipation, perspiration and preparation. Irrespective of the discipline, discomfort and discouragement at times, the end goal of success is worth every effort expended. If you don't believe me, ask the Lionesses.

Bearing that in mind, we must be personally prepared for the battles we will face – just like the Roman army, which was a formidable training force.

Paul's analogy, which draws upon the imagery of the Roman soldier, prompts us to put on God's armour every day. He warns us to be alert and to fully anticipate that we will be attacked. Indifference, slackness or laziness in preparing for battle is indefensible in the light of God's clarion call to arms.

But how do we do that? Consider this your personal training programme, a place for you to learn, reflect, prepare and act. One person's training plan may not work for everyone, so it is important to discover what works best for you. Together we will explore how you can stand up against the battles of 'the evil one', armed with the protective spiritual weaponry that God has provided. I trust that this workbook will offer fresh insights as we rediscover God's master plan for a successful spiritual breakthrough.

Your training programme

Use this workbook to journal, draw in, rip out and stick where you will see it every day. It is a practical resource that should help you to confidently wear your armour on a daily basis.

Remember: you are NOT alone in this. You are surrounded by an infinite army of God's fellow foot soldiers, and of course you have him. It is in God's strength, not our own, that we can daily stand on the front line.

On the next page we have outlined the practical steps we will use to put Scripture into practice. Each section provides opportunities to either share with other people or explore the ideas yourself.

LOOK what has come **BEFORE**	This section looks at verses and Bible stories to better understand each part of the armour of God.
WISE UP to now	This section provides questions and journalling prompts to help you reflect on your life now. You can write, draw or scribble, so grab a pen!
PREPARE for what is **AHEAD** (practical tasks for how to put it into practice)	This section offers practical tasks and creative activities to help you go deeper with each part of the armour.
MAKE MOVES with others and with God	This section is about remembering that you do not go alone. The tasks outlined here are focused on your giftings and accountability to others.
With all things **PRAY**	This section provides simple creative prayers you can use each day as you rise and dress in your armour.

Using this book in a group context

If you are using this book as a group:

- Read the LOOK BEFORE verses together and discuss what you think God might be saying through them, and how they link with the armour and your own life.

- Use the WISE UP questions as starting points for discussions as a group.

- Have a collective look at the creative tasks from PREPARE AHEAD. You might want to explore these in your time together.

- Complete the MAKE MOVES section when you are at home, and feed back the next time you meet.

Session 1 - The belt of truth

> 'Stand firm then, with the belt of truth buckled around your waist, with the breastplate of righteousness in place.'
>
> (Ephesians 6:14)

FACT: Did you know that belts were a sign of warrior prowess in ancient Italian culture? This is why warriors conspicuously wore broad decorated belts (and why taking a defeated enemy's belt was a worthy trophy). It is why gladiators and Roman soldiers wore them too.

Roman soldiers' belts were elaborately decorated with metal plates, sometimes with enamel and silver inlays. Belts seem to have been so associated with the Roman virtues of maleness and military prowess that making soldiers parade without their belts as a punishment was a great humiliation for them.[1]

You couldn't make it up!

Truth is defined as 'the actual state of a matter', 'conformity with reality', 'actuality', or 'a verified or indisputable fact'.[2] However, many theologians and social commentators would agree that we now live in a post-truth world. This describes a situation where Christianity is no longer the dominant civil religion of a society, and it has, over time, gradually assimilated values, culture and worldviews not necessarily described as Christian. In other words, there are no absolutes; rather it is your perspective, experience and ultimate conclusions that matter: my truth is mine and your truth is yours. To defer to absolutes is to declare to your contemporaries that you may be unenlightened, naive or uninformed.

---

1   See: **https://www.quora.com/Why-did-Roman-soldiers-wear-belts?** (accessed 3 November 2023).
2   'Truth', Word Reference: **https://www.wordreference.com/definition/truth**.

Living in a post-truth world

Tom Stafford, in his article 'How liars create the "illusion of truth"',[3] says that repetition makes a fact seem truer, regardless of whether it is or not. In other words, repeat a lie often enough and it becomes the truth. However, to guard against this, he advocates the necessity of constantly double-checking the facts: 'If something sounds plausible is it because it really is true, or have we just been told that repeatedly?'

This is sobering and insightful. In our world where disinformation abounds, we need to check what is being repeated against the validity of God's word. This activity counteracts our innate propensity to believe Satan's lies which, when repeatedly whispered to our souls, leave us gullible, susceptible and spiritually weakened. In contrast, knowledge of God's word and the diligent application of his truth sets us free.

The belt of truth is the first piece of armour mentioned by Paul, and I'm certain this isn't a coincidence. The belt was perhaps the most important symbol of a Roman soldier. In some ways, it was even more important than armour or weapons which, unlike the belt, were not used daily. The military belt was a wide strip of leather with metal plaques attached to it. These plaques not only had an obvious decorative function, meant to show the wealth of the owner, but they also served to stiffen the leather so that the belt couldn't roll under the weight of the weapons hanging from it.

Interestingly, God's word is the very first place Satan chooses to challenge us. He did it at the very beginning with Adam and Eve, by sowing doubt in their minds: 'Did God really say...?'

Paul warns us to be aware of the schemes of the devil. Why? Because he uses the same methods again and again. His antipathy towards God is centred on those individuals who are redeemed, transformed and aligned with his Son, and his tactics are tested and honed from centuries of deployment against Christians. But here is the good news: every doubt, disbelief and piece of disinformation about God is counteracted by God's truth. First, there is the truth of the transformative power from death to life through Jesus and the transactional work of the cross. Second, there is the spiritual formation of the believer as, through the work of the Holy Spirit, we intentionally seek to align our lives with the truth revealed in the Scriptures (see 2 Timothy 3:16–17).

---

3 Tom Stafford, 'How liars create the "illusion of truth"', BBC Future, 2016, available at: https://www.bbc.com/future/article/20161026-how-liars-create-the-illusion-of-truth (accessed 3 November 2023).

⊚ Look Before

Use the verses below as further reading to understand more of what the Bible says about truth. There is space around them to add some of your own.

'Jesus answered, "I am the way and the truth and the life. No one comes to the Father except through me."'

(John 14:6)

'We are from God, and whoever knows God listens to us; but whoever is not from God does not listen to us. This is how we recognise the Spirit of truth and the spirit of falsehood.'

(1 John 4:6)

'All your words are true; all your righteous laws are eternal.'

(Psalm 119:160)

 **Wise Up**

Answer the questions in the space below. Ask God's Holy Spirit to prompt you with reminders of his truth as you write your ideas down.

Wise up to the lie

• What lies have you been told?

• What from God's truth counters them? (This can be moments from your past, testimony or verses that come to mind.)

⇨ Prepare Ahead

Sometimes the lies of the enemy hit us when we least expect it and we can feel quite disarmed. Although the armour of God is a metaphor, this practical activity provides something physical to keep with you at all times, to remind you of God's truth while going about your day-to-day life.

You will need:

• A thin piece of leather or thick string

Cut the string long enough to tie around your wrist.

Look back at the verses and memories you have written down about God's truth. Choose the ones that resonate with you most.

Speak each of these truths out loud. As you say them, tie a knot in the string as a sign to help you recall the verse or memory.

Once you have finished, each of the knots in your string will represent a truth from God. Tie it around your wrist as a prompt for when you encounter the enemy's lies in your day-to-day life.

𢏿 Make Moves

We have just looked at how it can affect us negatively if we repeat lies to ourselves, so this is about repeating God's truth to ourselves each day instead.

There are eight small boxes on the next page. Fill in the blank boxes with truths that mean something to you.

Once you have completed the boxes, cut them out and stick them somewhere you will see them every day, so you can repeat them to yourself. This could be a wallet, a mirror or a kitchen cupboard.

As you see them, let God's truth soak into your heart and mind.

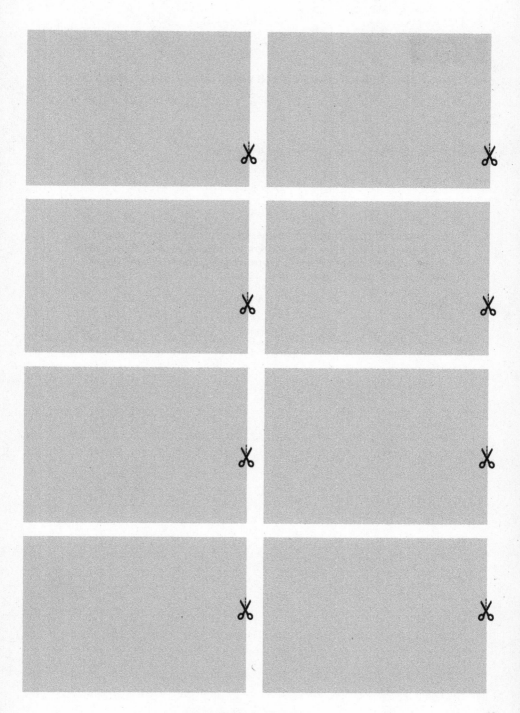

Pray

As you pray, place one hand where a belt would buckle and one hand on your heart.

Pause.

Breathe deeply into where your hands are placed.

Read this prayer aloud and slowly:

> *Lord,*
>
> *In a world of contradictions, may I ground myself in your truth.*
> *With the lies I am sold, may the knowledge of your truth override.*
> *In the haze of other people's 'truth', may I remember that Jesus is the way, the truth and the life.*
>
> *Amen*

Session 2
The breastplate of righteousness

'Stand firm then, with the belt of truth buckled around your waist, with the breastplate of righteousness in place.'

(Ephesians 6:14)

FACT: The breastplate of the Roman soldier consisted of metal formed to the shape of a man's chest, with a second piece fitted across the back. The breastplate served as protection for the most vital parts of the human body: the heart and lungs. The evolution of the *lorica segmentata* was a game-changer. This armour was essentially composed of numerous long straps of laminated iron, which were joined together either with metal hooks or with leather straps. Owing to its structure, this armour was flexible enough to enable easy movement of the torso. At the same time, the use of iron ensured maximum protection for those wearing it.

Did you know that, during the Second World War, the introduction of trench warfare and the devastating effects of artillery barrage armies led the German army to outfit soldiers in exposed positions with steel breastplates?

When was the last time you heard a sermon that had 'righteousness' and 'sin' as its primary subjects? Yet righteousness, as Paul advocates in Ephesians 6:14, is central to the transformation and spiritual formation of the Christian. And it's our sin, yours and mine, that prioritises righteousness as our rule of life. Righteousness as defined in Scripture simply means being in a right relationship with God. Just as the breastplate protected the vital organs of a Roman soldier, so righteousness, when twinned with truth, guards and protects the heart in our life with Christ.

We live in a world where people go about their lives according to what is right in their own eyes, basing their actions and reactions on whatever *they* think or feel is right. The belief that there is a standard set by God against which we are all accountable is an alien concept in today's postmodern, post-Christian world, and would probably be instantly dismissed as an outdated, irrelevant and deluded way of living. The fact that Paul likens righteousness to a breastplate, the single largest piece of protective equipment worn by the soldier, indicates that being in right standing with God is of utmost importance. He may well have been thinking about the words of Isaiah who, in reflecting on the pitiful spiritual state of the Israelites and their on–off relationship with God, said: 'All of us have become like one who is unclean, and all our righteous acts are like filthy rags... our sins sweep us away' (Isaiah 64:6). This echoes the sentiments of Romans 3:9–10 (MSG):

> So where does that put us? Do we Jews get a better break than the others? Not really. Basically, all of us, whether insiders or outsiders, start out in identical conditions, which is to say that we all start out as sinners. Scripture leaves no doubt about it: There's nobody living right, not even one.

The righteousness of man versus the righteousness of God

As a child I loved the fairy tale *The Emperor's New Clothes* by Hans Christian Andersen. It is the story of a vain emperor who is deceived by cunning swindlers posing as tailors. By pandering to the emperor's vanity and self-importance, they offer to custom-make him a magnificent outfit that will be invisible to those who are stupid or incompetent. When the conmen declare the outfit 'finished', they dress the emperor and he sets off in a public procession before the whole city. He walks proudly in full (false) confidence that he is exquisitely dressed. The crowd uncomfortably goes along with the pretence, not wanting to appear inept or stupid, until a child blurts out the truth – that the emperor is wearing nothing at all!

Righteousness is God's standard, prescribing how he navigates and interacts with us as his beloved children. It is an all-inclusive quality, including character (our nature), conscience (attitude), conduct (action) and command (word).

Much like the foolish emperor, we can be easily conned into believing that our good works constitute the fabric of our faith, and that it is the pursuit of noble activities – attending church, praying, reading the Bible, giving to charity – rather than our attentiveness to God that matters to him. We run the risk of parading our own self-importance, completely unaware that, spiritually speaking, we are either inadequately dressed or, worse, completely naked. Thank God for his Holy Spirit, who speaks truth to our heart, exposes our ineptitude and restores us if we so choose. 'As in water face reflects face, so the heart of man reflects the man' (Proverbs 27:19, ESV). Without truth, our righteousness will be based on our own attempts to impress God, instead of acknowledging that apart from him we can do nothing (John 15:5).

The only antidote to self-condemnation is for us to be clothed in Christ's righteousness. It is in Christ's victory alone that we are fully assured that the chasm between God's righteousness and our sinfulness has been bridged, and we can stand strong to face the enemy (1 Peter 3:18).

The breastplate as protection for our heart

Our spiritual growth is dependent upon the condition of our heart.

Most adults are aware of the importance of looking after their heart. In order to prevent a heart attack or stroke, we are advised to exercise, eat healthily and, where appropriate, have a check-up from time to time. Similarly, the Bible is clear that our heart health is critical to our spiritual well-being. The NIV refers to the heart over 500 times and the King James Version (KJV) more than 800 times. When the Scriptures talk about the heart, they are referring to it as the seat of our human emotion, mind, will and conscience (Hebrews 10:22; Proverbs 4:23; Acts 11:23; Matthew 9:4). Author Witness Lee explains: 'Our relationship with the Lord is always begun and maintained by the heart... for our heart is the gateway of our whole being.'[1] This is such an evocative image, and it leads us to better understand the role the heart plays in our growing intimacy and relationship with God. It is little wonder that our enemy, Satan, will prioritise the heart as his target.

Life throws up many issues and difficulties in our Christian walk, and these often surface first in our heart – that is, in our mind, emotion, will or conscience. As fallen human beings, it is relatively easy for us to become distracted, discouraged and distressed from the pressure of twenty-first-century living. It is no wonder that mental health and well-being is becoming the most talked-about issue and pursuit of our age. The breakneck speed at which we live our lives affords us little time to pause and reflect. 'Guard your heart above all else, for it determines the course of your life' (Proverbs 4:23, NLT).

Armour worn incorrectly does not function in the way it was intended, leaving the wearer vulnerable to severe or catastrophic injury. Likewise, there are several factors that can interfere with the effectiveness of our spiritual breastplate. Carelessness (1 Peter 5:8), unbelief (Hebrews 3:12) and disobedience (1 John 3:4) can hinder our ability to stand firm and minimise its power to protect us.

We 'put on' the breastplate of righteousness by intentionally seeking God and his ways above everything else (Matthew 6:33). The breastplate of righteousness has Christ's name stamped on it, as though he said, 'Your righteousness isn't sufficient to protect you. Wear mine.' As we yield ourselves to the process of change through the Holy Spirit, we become more attuned to hearing his voice, obeying his leading and submitting to him, allowing him to work in us. It is through our long obedience to moving in the same direction that we become conformed to the image of Christ and our choices become more aligned with God's will. Christ's righteousness, working through us, enables godly choices, sharpening our spiritual reflexes. In this way we quickly recognise and reject ideas, thoughts and temptations that come from the enemy and lead us *away* from God rather than *towards* him.

---

1 Witness Lee, The Economy of God *(California: Living Stream Ministry),* p. 75.

👁 Look Before

Use the verses below as further reading to understand more of what the Bible says about truth. There is space around the verses to add some of your own.

'For everyone has sinned; we all fall short of God's glorious standard. Yet God, in his grace, freely makes us right in his sight. He did this through Christ Jesus when he freed us from the penalty for our sins.'

(Romans 3:23–24, NLT)

'Run from anything that stimulates youthful lusts. Instead, pursue righteous living, faithfulness, love, and peace. Enjoy the companionship of those who call on the Lord with pure hearts.'

(2 Timothy 2:22, NLT)

'Remind the believers to submit to the government and its officers. They should be obedient, always ready to do what is good. They must not slander anyone and must avoid quarreling. Instead, they should be gentle and show true humility to everyone.

Once we, too, were foolish and disobedient. We were misled and became slaves to many lusts and pleasures. Our lives were full of evil and envy, and we hated each other. But—

When God our Savior revealed his kindness and love, he saved us, not because of the righteous things we had done, but because of his mercy. He washed away our sins, giving us a new birth and new life through the Holy Spirit. He generously poured out the Spirit upon us through Jesus Christ our Savior. Because of his grace he made us right in his sight and gave us confidence that we will inherit eternal life.'

(Titus 3:1–7, NLT)

Wise Up

Use the spaces below to write or draw freely as you answer these questions.

- **What are the things in your life that compromise your breastplate of righteousness?**

....

....

....

....

....

....

- **Do you have heart damage that interrupts your wisdom and moral judgement?**

....

....

....

....

....

- **What is God's truth that can restore your breastplate of righteousness?**

....

....

....

....

....

⇨ Prepare Ahead

The daily arrows that life throws at us are exactly what the breastplate of righteousness is designed to protect us against. Knowing what these arrows might be before we step out into our mission field is a key way to be prepared for daily life.

In our modern world, the enemy's arrows are often disguised as something totally normal, concealed by culture and 'the norm'. This could be money issues, the way we spend our time, consumerism or conversations about other people.

In the arrows below, write down the things you face in life, where the breastplate of righteousness protects you from making poor or misguided decisions.

Make Moves

Daily heart check

Keeping your heart healthy is a daily practice, but no matter how hard we try, things can sometimes affect us. Use this exercise each day to ask God to reveal areas where your heart has been damaged and where your breastplate of righteousness needs to be restored.

First, find somewhere quiet to be with God.

With one hand, find the pulse in your wrist or neck. Place the other hand on your chest.

Breathe deeply into your lungs and ask God's Holy Spirit to be present in you. Tune in to the rhythmical nature of your heart.

Say these words out loud as you tune in to your thoughts: 'Thank you, Lord, for my beating heart, which gives me life. Help me to guard it with your breastplate of righteousness. Prompt me about things in my heart that are slightly off from your navigating compass. Please, God, realign my vision so that you are my moral guide. Amen.'

Breathe deeply and release your hands.

Pray

As you pray, place one hand where your breastplate would sit and one hand on your heart.

Pause. Breathe deeply into where your hands are placed.

Read this prayer aloud and slowly:

> Lord,
>
> In a world of temptations, may I be guided towards what is right.
> When my heart is vulnerable, may it be guarded by your
> breastplate of righteousness.
>
> When I fall short, may I praise you for your grace through Jesus.
>
> Amen

Session 3 - Feet of readiness

'And with your feet fitted with the readiness that comes from the gospel of peace.'

(Ephesians 6:15)

> **FACT:** The Roman soldiers' footwear (*caligae*) were heavy-duty, thick-soled, open-work boots, sometimes crafted from a single piece of leather. The soles of the *caligae* were studded with hobnails. The open latticework design was subtly adjusted to fit the shape of the soldiers' feet.
>
> The hobnailed soles not only provided grip for the soldiers on uneven terrain, but when marching in unison with hundreds of fellow soldiers, they made a thunderous sound that must have been terrifying to the enemy.

Did you know that millions of people suffer from podophobia or petaphelaphobia? 'What is that?' I hear you cry. The terminology refers to an individual's fear of feet or the fear of people touching their feet. This fear may exhibit itself in physical discomfort and panic for sufferers, which can be debilitating.

Two thousand years ago, there were many reasons why feet would have been one of the most despised parts of the human body. Wearing sandals on the dusty, dirt-filled roads of Palestine in the first century AD made it imperative that feet were washed before a communal meal. This was especially the case because people reclined at low tables when eating, so their feet were very much on show. Indeed, the washing of feet was a humbling act of service and was a task relegated to household servants and slaves.

In referencing the military armour of the Roman soldier, Paul highlights the importance of his footwear. He would have been aware of the strenuous training regimen of the soldiers, who could march twenty miles a day, fully armed and equipped to fight on arrival. It was their preparedness and mobility that made them such a formidable fighting force.

What does he mean by 'feet fitted with the readiness that comes from the gospel of peace'? There are two ways to interpret this possibly ambiguous phrase. The Greek word *hetoimasia*, interpreted as 'readiness', can also mean 'preparation', 'equipment' or 'firmness'. Used here, it conveys the sense of 'readiness', as in enabling or equipping the Christian warrior to go forward, carrying the good news of peace to others. It echoes the words of Isaiah 52:7: 'How beautiful on the mountains are the feet of the messenger who brings good news, the good news of peace and salvation, the news that the God of Israel reigns!' (NLT).

Another interpretation of Ephesians 6:15 centres on readiness, as a 'prepared foundation' of knowledge and dependence on the gospel that infuses the Christian warrior with inner peace and confidence to progress Christ's mission in the world. It echoes 2 Timothy 4:2: 'Preach the word; be ready in season and out of season.' Both perspectives provide informative insights that deepen our understanding and faith.

Assume the position!

Reading from Ephesians 6:11–15, I am struck by the number of times Paul encourages the Ephesians (and us) to 'stand':

- So that you can take your stand against the devil's schemes;

- So that when the day of evil comes, you may be able to stand your ground;

- And after you have done everything, to stand;

- Stand firm then.

All seasoned marketing executives know that to make your audience take notice of your product or service, repetition of a word or an idea is vital. This is exactly what Paul is doing here. The repetitive use of the word 'stand' places emphasis on the Christian warrior assuming this position, which can be either an offensive or a defensive stance. Let us briefly examine both perspectives, as there is a richness in this word that lends itself to being explored further.

Mobility: to boldly go

There is no doubt that as witnesses of Christ and, as his foot soldiers and peacemakers, we too must be ready and prepared to bear witness to Jesus. Johannes Blauw has written: 'Missionary work is like a pair of sandals that have been given to the Church in order that it shall set out on the road and *keep on going*, to make known the mystery of the gospel.'[1]

---

1 Johannes Blauw, The Missionary Nature of the Church: A survey of the biblical theology of mission (Grand Rapids, Michigan: Eerdmans, 1974), p. 125.

Paul writes in Romans 10:13–15:

> 'Everyone who calls on the name of the Lord will be saved.' How, then, can they call on the one they have not believed in? And how can they believe in the one of whom they have not heard? And how can they hear without someone preaching to them? And how can anyone preach unless they are sent? As it is written, 'How beautiful are the feet of those who bring good news!'

To be sent, and to fulfil the mission we have been sent to accomplish, we must be sure that we are thoroughly equipped and prepared to do so. Donning the correct footwear is integral to our success.

The gospel of peace has always been good news to humankind. Indeed, peace is at the heart of what the gospel is all about. God, through Jesus Christ, has broken down the wall of division, or sin, that separated us from God. Accepting Jesus into our hearts and committing our lives to him enrols us on a journey of lifelong transformation, through God's Holy Spirit working in our innermost being. Being transformed by his word, we have peace with God and possess the peace of God, which establishes our identity as his beloved children, guards our hearts and minds (Philippians 4:4–7), and sets us apart from the potentially devastating impact of fear, worry and anxiety (John 14:1). As Clarence Haynes points out, the gospel of peace doesn't just stop with the living.[2] The gospel settles what happens after we die. Knowing that our eternity is secure produces an inexplicable peace that sets us free to live fruitfully and joyfully.

Immobility: to firmly stand

In his book *Christian Warfare and Spiritual Armour*, James Philip explains that Paul is making a critical point that footwear is to equip us to stand, not to walk or to run. Standing is the defensive position we should adopt: 'This part of the Christian armour... is to enable us to stand... firm, and not to panic or run away, knowing that the battle is not ours but God's. In other words, these sandals... are designed to keep the believer from getting cold feet!'[3] While they do not interfere with a soldier's mobility, their design, much like a climber's crampon, prevents the foot from slipping. It is a firm foundation.

The apostle Paul is clear that our fight and conflict is with the devil (Ephesians 6:12). Our stand, then, must be a defensive one, requiring us to guard against losing ground and being defeated by him. To adopt a solid stance we must be prepared to stand. It means being resolute and assured about what we are standing *on*, and confident and convinced of what we are standing *for*.

---

2   Clarence L. Haynes Jr, 'What Is the Gospel of Peace in the Armor of God?', Christianity.com, 22 August 2022, available at: **https://www.christianity.com/wiki/christian-terms/what-gospel-of-peace-in-armor-of-god.html** (accessed 3 November 2023).

3   James Philip, Christian Warfare and Armour (Pennsylvania: Victory Press, 1972), p. 51.

As a trainee manager in the NHS, I (Olivia) was under the supervision and mentorship of an experienced senior manager. It was my responsibility to glean as much useful information as I could from shadowing him, from observation and (where appropriate) from imitation. As a junior manager, I lacked confidence about how to end important meetings that I chaired, especially ones where conflict had surfaced. I noted how he handled this. Irrespective of whether the outcome of the meeting was favourable to his overall objectives, immediately at the meeting's end he would be the first to stand, signalling to all through his change of position that, from his perspective, all conversation had concluded and there was nothing further to add. He was neither impolite nor dismissive. However, his purposeful change of position, from seated to standing, communicated that *he* was in control and not the other way round. Participants would have to come to him if they wanted to engage further. Genius.

This is the mindset that we, as Christian warriors, need to adopt. The stance position is, of course, a metaphorical one, but it is illustrative of a position of commitment, not comfort. It is to plant your feet on the foundation of God's revealed truth to you, knowing (but not necessarily feeling) that you belong to him alone, that you are valued and that there is nothing, *nothing* that can separate you from his love (Romans 8:31–39). To stand for him is to pragmatically live and advance in this truth. It is a lifelong, daily commitment, to live obediently and sacrificially for him in the world (Titus 2:12).

◎ Look Before

Use the verses below as further reading to understand more of what the Bible says about truth. There is space around the verses to add some of your own.

'Jesus asked, "Do you finally believe? But the time is coming – indeed it's here now – when you will be scattered, each one going his own way, leaving me alone. Yet I am not alone because the Father is with me. I have told you all this so that you may have peace in me. Here on earth you will have many trials and sorrows. But take heart, because I have overcome the world."'

(John 16:31–33, NLT)

'"Everyone who calls on the name of the Lord will be saved." How, then, can they call on the one they have not believed in? And how can they believe in the one of whom they have not heard? And how can they hear without someone preaching to them? And how can anyone preach unless they are sent? As it is written, "How beautiful are the feet of those who bring good news!"'

(Romans 10:13–15)

'Don't worry about anything; instead, pray about everything. Tell God what you need, and thank him for all he has done. Then you will experience God's peace, which exceeds anything we can understand. His peace will guard your hearts and minds as you live in Christ Jesus.'

(Philippians 4:6–7, NLT)

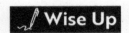
Wise Up

Reflect on these questions and write down your thoughts in the space below.

- Can you recall a time when God has given you peace in a hard situation you've found yourself in? Write an account, recalling the feelings you had at the time. If you are with other people, you can recount your story to them.

....

....

....

....

....

....

....

- Peace can often be viewed as a soft feeling, but the peace we hear about in the armour of God passage is explained as 'readiness', which shows that peace is not passive at all but a very active thing. Has there been a time when peace has given you an unexpected energy or readiness? Write or share these accounts.

....

....

....

....

....

....

....

....

⇨ Prepare Ahead

Peace is a confidence in the knowledge of what we already have and know in God as we step out in our lives with him. God offers a firm foundation for us to stand on and the confidence that he has already gone before us. The practical exercise below will help you to remember this as you leave your house each day.

You will need:

• A doormat (or the inside of a front door if you do not have a mat)

• A pen and Post-it note

Write the word 'peace' in bold or, if you like to draw, draw a set of sandals on a brightly coloured Post-it note. Stick this note by your doormat, or even on your front door, so that you see it as you leave the house.

Before you leave the house each day, stop and stand, feeling gravity pulling you down with a strong stance. Speak out these words: 'Lord, I stand firm in the knowledge that you have gone before me. I choose to walk through this door, my feet sandalled with the readiness of the gospel of peace. Amen.'

⋔ Make Moves

The storms of life can make it difficult to be at peace. However, God's supernatural peace surpasses any situation we are in, as long as we adopt the right posture of readiness in relation to his word.

This exercise is about sharing with other people the verses that resonate with you, and preparing ahead before you step out.

You will need:

• A pen and Post-it notes

In the footprint below, write as many verses as you can think of in the gospel about peace. You could share your favourite verse with another person to create a larger collection.

Pick the verse that most rings true to you and write it on a Post-it. Speak it out loud as you write it out.

Now stick the Post-it note next to the place where you keep your shoes. That way you can read it as you physically put on your shoes, to remind you you're not walking alone.

Finally, pick the shoes you wear most and turn them over so you can see the soles. Using your pen, write the word 'Peace' on the sole. (You may not want to do this bit, as it will mark your shoes! However, I encourage you to find a way to step out of your door with peace physically accompanying you, to remind you of God's presence as you find yourself in the storms of life.)

Say this prayer:

Lord,

Help me to prepare myself for what's ahead by always knowing your peace. Help me to stand firm in readiness to 'go', carrying the gospel of peace each day. May that peace transfer to others as I encounter them.

Amen

As you walk in your shoes you will carry peace with you and leave it behind you – both physically and spiritually.

Pray

As you pray, place both of your feet flat on the floor, feeling the pull of gravity, and place one hand on your heart.

Pause.

Breathe deeply into where your hand is placed.

Read this prayer aloud and slowly:

> *Lord,*
>
> *When the ground feels unsteady, may I stand firmly in your peace.*
>
> *When I am called to move, may I walk boldly, knowing you have already won.*
>
> *When I feel insecure, may I know that nothing separates me from God's love.*
>
> *Amen*

Session 4 - The shield of faith

'In addition to all this, take up the shield of faith, with which you can extinguish all the flaming arrows of the evil one.'

(Ephesians 6:16)

FACT: The shield, or *scutum*, of the Roman soldier was a large, curved rectangular shield made from wood and weighing about 10 kg (22 lb). It was light enough to be held in one hand, leaving the other free to engage in fighting. Its vast height and width largely covered the soldier's body, making it very unlikely for him to be hit by missile fire or be mortally wounded in hand-to-hand combat. At the centre of the shield was a rounded iron protrusion, or 'boss', that also served as a punching weapon or to push back the enemy.

The description of the shield of faith in Paul's statement stands out from the other aspects. It not only takes central position in this catalogue of Christian armour, with three parts mentioned before and three after, but it is also the one piece of armour where Paul describes its function as well as the result of its proper use! By making the shield the focus, he intimates the vital importance of it.

This is further emphasised by the introductory words 'above all' (KJV) used to introduce this piece of equipment. As James Philip notes, the shield is a moveable commodity.[1] It can be shifted to cover the various parts of the body that are already protected by armour. In effect, this shield provides double armour. This is an illuminating picture and helps to get to the heart of the message Paul is trying to convey. Essentially, what is the use of truth, righteousness, the gospel of peace and so on if we do not have faith? Faith is the shield.

The nature of faith as a shield

The Greek word for shield, *thyreós*, means 'gate' or 'door-shaped', and it is used to describe the large, oblong, ancient Roman shield which looked like a full door and was large enough to provide full protection from attack. Interestingly, it is only used here in Ephesians 6:16.

---

1   James Philip, Christian Warfare and Armour *(Pennsylvania: Victory Press, 1972), p. 67.*

It may be useful to revisit the definition of faith to understand why it is integral to our defence and why we need to be armed with it. Faith, as defined by the Scriptures, is more than 'belief in God', which is the most common use of the term today. For example, we may say, 'I have come to faith,' meaning that we have now come to a belief in God. But it is much more than this. Faith, as defined in Hebrews 11:1, means a reliance on God, as well as being completely assured by him. *The Thematic NIV Study Bible* defines faith as 'a constant outlook of trust towards God, whereby human beings abandon all reliance on their efforts and put their full confidence in him, his word and his promises'.[2] The shield of faith, then, is the shield that faith provides. Faith *is* the shield. So how do we use the shield to its most powerful effect?

Fighting fire with fire: the nature of fiery darts

Conversations about Satan or the devil are often perceived as outdated in our modern world. For many Christians, this subject is not popular, studied or preached about, so it is unsurprising that we tend to gloss over it. However, Paul clarifies both the importance and the use of the shield of faith as an effective weapon against Satan's duplicity.

Paul's reference to the 'flaming arrows of the evil one' is an explicit indication that Satan has waged war on believers and targets us for his attacks (flaming arrows). In Paul's time, the arrow was made from a hollow reed filled with a flammable liquid, with its tip soaked and wrapped in fabric so it would burn with hot, angry flames. In ancient Roman warfare, arrows or darts were ignited and fired against the enemy to produce maximum damage. The characteristics of these arrows were their swiftness, their unexpectedness, their immediate effect and their deadliness in piercing as well as setting their target on fire.

Many of us will have experienced the effect of Satan's flaming arrows, even though we may not have recognised their origin. These can take the form of sudden dark or blasphemous thoughts, despair, rejection, pride, fear, distraction, malicious thoughts and so many other things, too numerous to mention here. Quite often, these arrows are fired at us at unexpected times and places, including when we are occupied in spiritual activities. The enemy's strategy is to have us believe that these thoughts and associated feelings originate in ourselves and, as a consequence, we are unworthy, unspiritual beings who have no right to be called Christians at all. The feelings of inner despair that we experience at these times

---

2   Alister McGrath (ed.), The Thematic NIV Study Bible *(London: Hodder & Stoughton, 1996).*

can be disarming and disorientating, leaving us doubting the faithfulness of God and questioning his love for us. Counteracting this disabling position would be impossible without God's help.

The phrase 'with which you can' uses the Greek word *dunamis*, which denotes explosive or dynamic power. This strengthens the depth of this verse, so that Ephesians 6:16 could actually be translated: 'Above all, taking the shield of faith, by which you will be dynamically empowered.' This rephrasing helps us to understand that it is God's Holy Spirit that gives us the power to stand against the enemy. We don't face him or his tactics alone. The Holy Spirit supercharges our shield!

How to use the shield of faith to extinguish *all* the fiery darts of the evil one

A shield, whether physical or spiritual, can only be effective when it is raised. This requires an ongoing state of preparedness and participation on our part (1 Peter 5:8–9).

The practical application means that our faith always points us to God; to his character, his promises and his activity, not ours. We tend to look inwards in a futile effort to cultivate a faith that is largely self-centred and ineffective because it originates in human effort.

Just as the shield of the Roman soldier was covered with canvas and leather, which could be doused with water to protect against flaming arrows, rendering them harmless, we too are to immerse ourselves in the word and promises of God, because they enable us to extinguish all the flaming arrows of the enemy.

This was the strategy Jesus used when, early in his ministry, he was besieged by Satan during his forty-day fast in the wilderness. Jesus' reliance on the word of God – quoting it, explaining it and defending it all through his ministry – set a pattern that we can imitate in our Christian journey. Being adept at handling the word necessitates us being intentional in reading and studying it, so we can be prepared and ready to use it whenever the need arises.

Faith, then, is the defensive and protective barrier that exposes and mitigates the schemes of Satan. When we believe in God and are fully assured of his promises as revealed in his word, we remain grounded in truth, and the lies and deceptiveness of the enemy lose their power. This is what victory looks like, and all believers have this promise.

👁 Look Before

Use the verses below as further reading to understand more of what the Bible says about truth. There is space around the verses to add some of your own.

'Pray, too, that we will be rescued from wicked and evil people, for not everyone is a believer. But the Lord is faithful; he will strengthen you and guard you from the evil one. And we are confident in the Lord that you are doing and will continue to do the things we commanded you. May the Lord lead your hearts into a full understanding and expression of the love of God and the patient endurance that comes from Christ.'

(2 Thessalonians 3:2–5, NLT)

'David sang this song to the LORD on the day the LORD rescued him from all his enemies and from Saul. He sang:

"The LORD is my rock, my fortress, and my savior;
    my God is my rock, in whom I find protection.
He is my shield, the power that saves me,
    and my place of safety.
He is my refuge, my savior,
    the one who saves me from violence.
I called on the LORD, who is worthy of praise,
    and he saved me from my enemies."'

(2 Samuel 22:1–4, NLT)

'So be strong and courageous! Do not be afraid and do not panic before them. For the LORD your God will personally go ahead of you. He will neither fail you nor abandon you.'

(Deuteronomy 31:6, NLT)

Wise Up

Reflect on the questions below and write down your thoughts in the spaces provided.

- **Has there been a time in your past when the shield of faith protected you against the enemy?**

....

....

....

....

....

- **Has there been a time when you felt your grip on the shield of faith weaken? How did you find strength?**

....

....

....

....

....

- **What arrows do you feel Satan throws at you, and how do they attack your weaknesses? How does faith counter these?**

....

....

....

....

....

....

- **Which scriptures help you to keep your faith in God?**

....

....

....

....

....

....

⇨ Prepare Ahead

When the Roman army was advancing into battle, the flaming arrows were often used as a distraction tactic to confuse the soldiers enough for the impenetrable wall of defence they had created to be broken. The amount of training the army went through, however, meant that even if this happened, the soldiers' muscle memory would quickly help them to remain in formation.

We can achieve this by memorising Bible verses. Having Scripture memorised means that when our faith is shaken, we can, without hesitation, draw strength from the verses we know and have built our foundation on.

Use the space below to write a short verse that reminds you of God's promises.

Repeat the process by writing the verse multiple times.

Speak the verse out loud as you write, but each time you copy the verse, leave a word out.

The process will finish with you being able to say the verse out loud without needing the writing as a prompt at all.

Use this verse as a shield as you repeat it each day.

🫂 Make Moves

The Roman army would hold their shields together in different formations to create an 'impenetrable wall' as they advanced into battle.

It is the same for us as Christians! We are an army together, not alone. And our faith shields are supposed to be used together.

Sometimes we may have a flaming arrow thrown at us that causes confusion or hurt, or challenges our faith. This is where we can rely on those around us and our knowledge of God's promises to protect us as we go forward!

The image below shows multiple Roman shields in their impenetrable wall formation. In the centre of each shield, write the name of a person who helps you to stay strong in your faith – someone you lean on in the hard times. You may also choose to write a verse or memory of God's faithfulness in your life in one of the shields, to help strengthen your faith.

Pray

As you pray, hold one arm out in front of your body to symbolise protection and place one hand on your heart.

Pause.

Breathe deeply into where your hands are placed.

Read this prayer aloud and slowly:

> *Lord,*
>
> *When arrows come my way, may I confidently lift my shield of faith.*
>
> *In times when my faith is shaken, may your word strengthen my faith in you.*
>
> *When I feel as though I am alone, may I remember those who hold their shields next to mine.*
>
> *Amen*

Session 5 – The helmet of salvation

> 'Take the helmet of salvation and the sword of the Spirit, which is the word of God.'
>
> (Ephesians 6:17)

FACT: Roman soldiers used a wide range of helmets, and throughout the history of the Roman Empire, helmet styles evolved and changed. The Roman helmet (*galea*) served two main purposes: protection and identification.

The style of helmet that was popular during the first century AD (the time Paul was writing) was crafted from brass or bronze, and featured neck and cheek guards to protect the vital areas of the head, neck and face. Helmets worn by legionaries and centurions had crests with plumes of horsehair, which were usually dyed red to make them easily identifiable in battle.

Timothy Gallwey's book, *'The Inner Game of Tennis'*,[1] is not just about the game of tennis but focuses especially on the inner struggle we all face in performing at our best. The book's premise is this: the biggest obstacles we face in achieving performance excellence are often our self-doubt, self-criticism and negative thinking. Gallwey advocates that our tendency towards negative self-talk can hinder our ability to access our natural strengths, making us distracted, anxious and hesitant. I understand Gallwey's hypothesis.

As a budding athlete trying to find the track-and-field discipline I was best suited to, I (Olivia) remember trying out for the 400 x 400 hurdles. Despite being quite an accomplished sprinter, I knocked over every hurdle at every attempt. I knew the reasons for my poor performance. Despite understanding the technique to seamlessly combine sprinting and jumping to maximum effect, it felt too hard, so I had 'checked out' in my mind. The failure was initialised in my head a long time before it was validated in my athletic performance.

Of course, an anecdote can only go so far. In writing to the Ephesians about the helmet of salvation, Paul is advocating much more than the power of positive thinking. He is prompting the early Christians to be armed with a mindset that is

---

1 Timothy Gallwey, The Inner Game of Tennis (London: Pan, 2015).

God-focused and Holy Spirit-empowered. He is proclaiming that the assurance of salvation is our impenetrable defence against anything the enemy throws at us, because the mind presents the perfect arena for Satan to showcase his activity. Paul understands the practical outworking of Proverbs 23:7, which says, 'For as he thinks within himself, so he is' (NASB). Just as it would be unthinkable for a Roman soldier to go into battle without his head protected, so the spiritual application of the helmet is obvious. Paul is drawing attention to the necessity of the Christian protecting the head – the mind, emotions and intellect that reflect our whole position as Christians. The helmet of salvation as a visual metaphor serves us in two ways: identity and protection.

It was Henry Ford, the American pioneer and industrialist, who said, 'Whether you think you can, or you think you can't, you're right.' His words articulate the fact that our mind and thoughts largely determine how we perceive ourselves, interpret the world around us and construct our responsive behaviours accordingly.

The helmet of salvation as our protection

The helmet helps to protect and guard us against false teaching and the deceptive tactics of the enemy. One way that Satan attacks us is by undermining the foundations of our faith, eroding the assurance of our salvation. I (Olivia) remember well, as a young, immature Christian, how easy it was for me to believe I had 'lost' my salvation when I made mistakes, exercised poor judgement and was not (in my opinion at least) obedient to God. I acted as both judge and jury, and condemned myself as unworthy, sinful and almost unredeemable. I cannot recall how many times I convinced myself I had committed the unpardonable sin mentioned in Matthew 12:31.

You may have been in that place too. Growing in maturity in the Christian faith does not render us immune to these deceptions. We are warned in the Scriptures to be alert and of sober mind as the enemy prowls like a roaring lion, seeking someone to devour (1 Peter 5:8). Unsound and misguided thinking about God and the transformative work of salvation in our lives leaves us prey to the enemy in a similar way to a soldier engaging in deadly warfare without the protection of a helmet. To be unprotected in this way allows us to make decisions that are swayed by our emotions and the lies of the enemy rather than based on the truth of God's word.

The helmet of salvation is our identification

These are interesting times for the study of identity. Our contemporary world asks us to choose an identity to fit the person we believe ourselves to be. This includes choosing our gender, or identifying ourselves with whatever it is that takes our fancy or aligns with our personal values, ethos and beliefs.

The helmet of salvation reminds us of our identity in Christ. It gives us hope and confidence in the victory that Jesus has already won for us. It removes the temptation for us to build our own identity based on our efforts and what we accomplish, and therefore how we see ourselves. Alternatively, our true identity as followers of Christ is based on what he has done for us, what he has accomplished as the redeemer of our souls and how he now sees us. Understanding this truth catapults us straight into the place of victory – not because we have it all worked out in our heads, but because he has already done the hard work for us.

We now have a new identity that Satan instantly recognises, but because we readily believe the lies that he feeds us, we are susceptible to his subtlety and deviousness. For this reason, God reminds us constantly, through his word and the inner witness of his Holy Spirit, that in Christ we are loved, chosen, forgiven, redeemed, adopted and therefore heirs and joint heirs with him. In our day-to-day living we, through him, are more than conquerors and inseparable from the love of God that is in Christ Jesus our Lord (Romans 8:37–39). As Brené Brown explains: 'What we know matters, but who we are matters more.'[2]

How do we put on the helmet of salvation?

As a young mum to my toddler son Josh, when he asked me about Father Christmas one year, I (Olivia) decided to inform him, then and there, that Father Christmas, flying reindeer and elves did not exist. Please don't judge me. My rationale was that I wanted him to know the truth as early as possible to accommodate his bitter disappointment that his mum was the one who granted his Christmas wishes. I adopted the same protocol with the tooth fairy! There is such an innate, endearing quality about children and their belief system. Jesus used them to illustrate the heart posture that adults should emulate (Matthew 18:2–4). As John Piper puts it: 'Trust like a child. Think like a man [or woman].'[3]

---

2 Brené Brown, Daring Greatly: How the courage to be vulnerable transforms the way we live, love, parent, and lead (London: Penguin, 2013).
3 John Piper, 'Childlike, Not Childish', Desiring God, available at: https://www.desiringgod.org/interviews/childlike-not-childish (accessed 3 November 2023).

Mature thinking

As Christians, putting on the helmet of salvation is to embrace sound, mature thinking. This means we need to embrace, in much the same way a young child does, the fact that God is in charge and in ultimate control – even when every sense and sinew points to a contrary belief.

Romans 12:2 reminds us that our minds need to be constantly renewed by exchanging the untruths that we have unwittingly assimilated for God's truths as revealed in his word. We need the empowering Holy Spirit to help us, working from the inside out, to rewire our mindset from one of rebellion and wilfulness to one that seeks to please him in our behaviours and actions. We will explore more about the power of God's word in the next chapter, which is about the sword of the Spirit.

👁 Look Before

Use the verses below as further reading to understand more of what the Bible says about truth. There is space around the verses to add some of your own.

'God saved you by his grace when you believed. And you can't take credit for this; it is a gift from God. Salvation is not a reward for the good things we have done, so none of us can boast about it. For we are God's masterpiece. He has created us anew in Christ Jesus, so we can do the good things he planned for us long ago.'

(Ephesians 2:8–10, NLT)

'Jesus told him, "I am the way, the truth, and the life. No one can come to the Father except through me. If you had really known me, you would know who my Father is. From now on, you do know him and have seen him!"'

(John 14:6–7, NLT)

'But forget all that –
  it is nothing compared to what I am going to do.
  For I am about to do something new
  See, I have already begun! Do you not see it?
  I will make a pathway through the wilderness.
  I will create rivers in the dry wasteland.'

(Isaiah 43:18–19, NLT)

 **Wise Up**

Reflect on these questions and write down your thoughts in the spaces provided.

- **How would you describe your identity? What does your identity in Christ mean in your life?**

....

....

....

....

....

- **What does it mean to be a child of God?**

....

....

....

....

....

- **What outside voices in your life, or recurring thoughts, do you feel compromise your knowledge of salvation?**

....

....

....

....

....

The phrase 'It's all in your head' is often seen as negative, but it shows us how much weight our minds can carry regarding our decisions. The head holds the brain – the control centre of the body. Which naturally means that our mind is the control centre of our soul!

Healthy mind = healthy soul

Below is a mind–check exercise. Use it to gauge the parts of your life where the enemy will see weakness and counter your knowledge of salvation. You may want to adapt the scale to best suit your situation.

Mark where you are now, then where you want to ask God to help you to be.

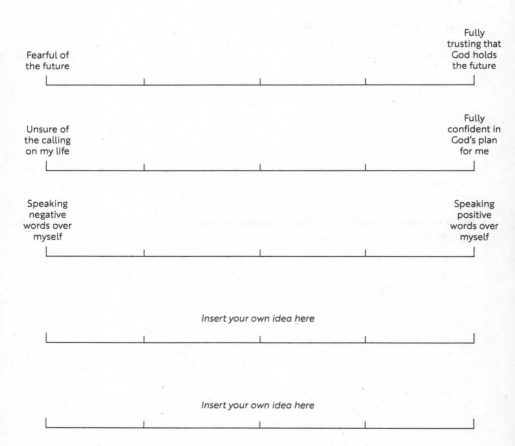

Fearful of
the future

Fully
trusting that
God holds
the future

Unsure of
the calling
on my life

Fully
confident in
God's plan
for me

Speaking
negative
words over
myself

Speaking
positive
words over
myself

Insert your own idea here

Insert your own idea here

👥 Make Moves

In order for the Roman army to be as strong as possible, its soldiers needed to unlearn bad habits when it came to wearing armour, preparing for battle and advancing. Our brains create neurological pathways that control our body and mind. However, research has shown that we have the ability, with a bit of work, to rewire those pathways.

We might have many unhealthy thought patterns, lies of the devil, that we need to undo, and we need to fully wear the helmet of salvation to protect our thoughts.

With another person, or by yourself in a quiet moment, bring to mind the lies you have spoken over yourself, the false identity you might have picked up that God hasn't given you. Quite often these begin with an 'un' – unforgivable, unloved, unintelligent, unheard – and they are *not* what God calls us.

Write them in the first column below.

In the second column, write truths that you know God has spoken over you. There are a few verses in place to get you started. These verses are the truth, and are the helmet of salvation that God gives us to wear each day.

Undo	Make True
	I am God's masterpiece (Ephesians 2:10)
	God is with me wherever I go (Joshua 1:9)
	I am so loved by God (1 John 4:9–10)

Pray

As you pray, place one hand firmly on your head and the other on your heart.

Pause.

Breathe deeply into where your hands are placed.

Read this prayer aloud and slowly:

> *Lord,*
>
> *When the foundations of my faith are attacked, may the helmet of salvation protect my mind.*
>
> *When my identity is challenged, may I recognise that it is rooted in Christ.*
>
> *In times when my thoughts are shaken, may I know that God is sovereign, in charge and in control.*
>
> *Amen*

Session 6 - The sword of the Spirit

'Take the helmet of salvation and the sword of the Spirit, which is the word of God.'

(Ephesians 6:17)

FACT: The Roman sword, or gladius, is one of the most widely recognised swords of any culture. The fighting skills and rigorous training of the Roman soldier made the sword a deadly weapon, and this skilled use of it was one of the major factors behind their long and successful military reign. The Romans used the knowledge gained from other cultures to create a sword suitable for any military situation they encountered: short swords for close combat and longer swords suited for horseback combat.

The most commonly used sword was the short sword – a 20-inch, double-edged blade with a diamond-shaped tip. This sword became known as 'the sword that conquered the world'. This was because the short length allowed the soldier to come very close to the enemy, inside his guard, and thrust it in any direction at a deadly pace.

The sword is both an offensive and a defensive weapon. The skilled soldier would use the shield and the sword to advance against the enemy, stepping into the enemy's space with the sole purpose of inflicting a fatal wound.

Paul is very clear about the sword of the Spirit and what it represents to the Christian, defining it as the word of God. The Greek 'word of God' here is not the usual word we have in the New Testament, *Logos* (John 1:1), but the word *rhema*. The word *rhema* means 'utterance' and refers to the spoken word. Paul is stating that the sword of the Spirit is not just the written word of God, but is also the written word of God that is *spoken directly into the situation or conflict* someone is facing.

Understanding this is empowering and has a huge impact. Speaking God's word is an effective and powerful weapon that changes the situation every single time. Many women and men have served their country through the military and are trained and prepared to sacrificially defend it with their lives. But how many of us realise that we too are engaged in a daily real-life battle against the deadliest of enemies, Satan, whose mission to kill, steal and destroy is an unrelenting one? In this battle, we must be prepared and agile enough to defend, as well as to move into offensive positions, when warranted. The sword of the Spirit is a crucial weapon in these situations.

The sword as a defensive weapon

We must understand the connection between the sword and the word of God. God's word is dynamic, alive and active (Hebrews 4:12). Through God's word, we learn to distinguish right from wrong, using it as the ultimate truth, and we are to become proficient in it. Like a soldier who is responsible for ensuring that his weapons are battleworthy, we too have to take the necessary time to sharpen our swords.

If we're lacking in knowledge of God's word, we are left vulnerable to Satan's attack. We will struggle to make headway and will suffer defeat. But we build our faith as we learn to trust God and *his* version of events rather than ours. Proverbs 3:5 advises us: 'Trust in the LORD with all your heart; do not depend on your own understanding' (NLT). Such trust *always* starts from a place of relationship. It is only by becoming intimately acquainted with him that we grow, learning how to apply his word directly and with laser focus to the situation or circumstance.

The sword as an offensive weapon

The word of God not only has the power to change *our* lives; it can also change the lives of others. God, through his Spirit, works in us to advance and occupy new territories. This is powerfully captured in the Acts account of the birth of the Church through the outpouring of the Holy Spirit. This resulted in thousands hearing the good news of hope and salvation.

We are on the offensive when we appropriately share God's word, testifying to his goodness, especially with those who have never heard about Jesus. We can do this anytime and anywhere, reaching the people within our sphere of influence. In a court of law, a witness is required only to testify to what they have seen and experienced. Their testimony does not draw upon speculation, nor are they asked for a personal interpretation of the events. They are only required to state the facts. Likewise, when we share our personal stories of encounters with God, it is the hearer who determines their response to what we have shared. This relieves us of the pressure and anxiety of being 'gospel salespersons' in search of quick results. Rather, we leave the outcome to God as he does what only he can do, making the word come alive in the hearts and minds of those with whom we share (Isaiah 55:11).

Trained to fight

The Roman army was a formidable fighting force. Its soldiers were exceptionally well trained and disciplined. Their agile battle manoeuvres meant that the sword and the shield were used to maximum effect, their huge shields covering half the body and the sword ready to protect the other half. The sharp pointed tip of the sword was a more proficient fighting weapon than the arm's-length swords of their opponents.

When Paul talks about putting on the whole armour of God, he is emphasising that the Christian is actively engaged in the fight of their life against a formidable, unseen foe. We too must learn to be intentional participants in building our spiritual proficiency, allowing the message of Christ to dwell in us richly (Colossians 3:6).

There are innumerable ways for us to become familiar with God's word. So how do we train ourselves to do this? The acronym TRAIN might be useful here.

Time
We have to be intentional about this. We need to carve out time to listen to, read and reflect on God's word daily.

Read
We need to read Scripture mindfully, reflectively and imaginatively, so that we are wholly engaged in understanding what God is saying to us.

Ask
'Why', 'what', 'who' and 'how' are great words to begin a question relating to the Scripture we have read. For example: What is God saying here? Who is he speaking to? Why is this important? What is he saying to me? How should I respond?

Invite
We then invite God's Holy Spirit to reveal his will to us as we read the Scriptures.

Next
What needs to be done next as a result of working through the steps above? Do we need to repent of a revealed sin or make an action plan?

The basis of our faith and our growing relationship with God rest unreservedly upon his living, powerful and dynamic word to us.

◎ Look Before

Use the verses below as further reading to understand more of what the Bible says about truth. There is space around the verses to add some of your own.

'Do not take revenge, my dear friends, but leave room for God's wrath, for it is written: "It is mine to avenge; I will repay," says the Lord. On the contrary:

"If your enemy is hungry, feed him;
    if he is thirsty, give him something to drink.
In doing this, you will heap burning coals on his head."

Do not be overcome by evil, but overcome evil with good.'

(Romans 12:19–21)

'Then Jesus was led by the Spirit into the wilderness to be tempted by the devil. After fasting for forty days and forty nights, he was hungry. The tempter came to him and said, "If you are the Son of God, tell these stones to become bread."

Jesus answered, "It is written: 'Man shall not live on bread alone, but on every word that comes from the mouth of God.'"

Then the devil took him to the holy city and set him on the highest point of the temple. "If you are the Son of God," he said, "throw yourself down. For it is written:

"'He will command his angels concerning you,
    and they will lift you up in their hands,
        so that you will not strike your foot against a stone.'"

Jesus answered him, "It is also written: 'Do not put the Lord your God to the test.'"

Again, the devil took him to a very high mountain and showed him all the kingdoms of the world and their splendour. "All this I will give you," he said, "if you will bow down and worship me."

Jesus said to him, "Away from me, Satan! For it is written: 'Worship the Lord your God, and serve him only.'"

Then the devil left him, and angels came and attended him.'

(Matthew 4:1–11)

Questions on using God's word

Reflect on these questions and write down your thoughts in the spaces provided.

- **Which verses or stories from the Bible have been important to you when faced with challenges or opposition?**

....

....

....

....

....

- **Can you remember a time when you used the word of God as a weapon against the enemy?**

....

....

....

....

- **In what ways would you like to strengthen your knowledge of Scripture to help in your daily battles?**

....

....

....

....

....

⇨ Prepare Ahead

The enemy was sly when he approached Jesus in the wilderness. Jesus was alone after a long stretch without food and comforts, and without his Father, meaning he was probably at one of his weakest points. Still, when Satan came to Jesus, hoping he would be vulnerable, Jesus used the greatest weapon he had against temptation from the enemy: Scripture.

We are often at our most vulnerable when we are alone. In moments of weakness, Satan tries his best to come for us. Like Jesus, it is important that we have our sword at the ready.

For the following task to work, you need to be disciplined and rigorous in your practice each day.

Pick three short verses you do not yet know by heart that highlight the following:

- **what God says about you;**

- **God's plan for you;**

- **the salvation God gives you.**

Each morning, read over these verses. Say them out loud three times.

Repeat this process every day until you are able to recite them by heart.

Once you are able to do that, pick three more verses and start the process again.

God has already won the battle! We know the ending, which gives us incredible strength. However, speaking Scripture out loud holds power. Knowing these scriptures by heart gives us even more strength against the enemy in our daily lives.

👥 Make Moves

'For where two or three gather in my name, there am I with them.'
(Matthew 18:20)

There is so much power in diving into God's word together with other people. This is simply about accountability to others. By reading God's word together, it encourages us to learn from each other and not to fall at the first hurdle.

Try putting time aside each week to study Scripture with others. If you can't physically get together, why not commit to reading a book of the Bible together and chatting over the phone about it?

Accountability is key!

🙏 Pray

As you pray, hold one hand in a fist in front of your body, as if brandishing a sword, and place the other hand on your heart.

Pause.

Breathe deeply into where your hands are placed.

Read this prayer aloud and slowly:

Lord,

When I am vulnerable to attack, may I be prompted by your word, by the Holy Spirit.

When I advance into new territories, may you work through me by your Holy Spirit.

When I feel threatened and tempted, may your Holy Spirit bring your word quickly to my mind.

Amen

Session 7 - Pray in the Spirit

> 'And pray in the Spirit on all occasions with all kinds of prayers and requests. With this in mind, be alert and always keep on praying for all the Lord's people.'
>
> (Ephesians 6:18)

Prayer is different for everyone. Some people will pray in pictures, some with words, some while they walk and some in the stillness of the early morning. However we connect with God, we are called to always be alert, and to keep praying for each other and in the Spirit on all occasions.

Below are some simple ideas and activities to help you pray in different creative ways. They can be adapted for any situation and may prompt you to pray throughout your day.

Praying *on* the armour

Here are some words from Jo, a friend of Martha's and a wonderful disciple of Jesus, on her personal prayer and the armour of God:

I imagine myself putting on the armour of God before I go to sleep. I put on a belt, the breastplate, etc. I put the shield up in front of me and draw the sword of the Spirit. When I feel unhelpful, horrible thoughts coming at me, I imagine myself hiding behind the shield – it protects me from nasty thoughts. Sometimes I use the sword to cut down bad thoughts. I find it really helps me take control of my thoughts at bedtime or in the wee small hours of the morning!

Jo's way of visualising the physical armour of God is a powerful reminder of God's protection every day.

Try using this visualisation yourself. As you go through each part of the armour, really picture yourself putting on that heavy-duty protection. Ask God to give you the element you need at the end of the day or for the day ahead.

Jam-jar prayer

This is a very simple prayer idea to help you to pray for different people throughout your week.

You will need:

- A jar or pot
- Some lolly sticks or pieces of paper
- A pen

Before you begin this task, ask God to bring to your mind people for you to pray for. These may be family or friends, people you have said you will be praying for or people who just pop into your head.

Write their names on your small pieces of paper or lolly sticks.

Leave the jar somewhere in your house where you will see it often: by the kettle, next to your toothbrush, on your desk, by your bed...

Each time you see the jar, pull one of the names out and take a moment or two to pray for that person. Ask God to fill them with his Holy Spirit as they walk through their day.

Breath prayer

This prayer offers a moment in which to ask God to be present in our world.

Stop and bring your attention to your breathing.

Intentionally slow your breathing down.

As you breathe out, think of something you would like to ask God to help you get rid of.

As you breathe in, ask God to fill you with something you would like to have more of. For example:

> Breathe out: 'Lord, take away my fear for the future.'
> Breathe in: 'Lord, fill my soul with peace.'
> Breathe out: 'Fear.'
> Breathe in: 'Peace.'

Ending

All new beginnings start with an ending.

As Christ's followers, we are forearmed with great news. It is that the victory has already been won through Christ who strengthens us through the Holy Spirit and never leaves us to fight our battles alone. We trust that this study and its practical applications have been insightful and useful to you.

Be bold. Take courage. Trust God.

Now it begins... and the end will be glorious.

About the authors

Olivia Amartey is executive director for the Elim Pentecostal Church, having previously worked in senior leadership positions within the NHS. She is also associate pastor of Crosspoint Church, a church plant based in north Birmingham, and has a passion for sharing God's word creatively. Much appreciated for her sense of fun, Olivia was a lively contributor to David Wilbourne's well-received York Course, *You Can Be Serious!* (2023), and the upcoming 2024 York Course, *The Gift of Christ*.

Martha Shrimpton is an actor–musician and presenter who has worked within the arts for a number of years. She is the director of Nimbus Collective, which encourages individuals and churches to connect with God in creative ways by producing resources, hosting events and leading training days. She is also the author of *Wow! Jesus* and *Wow! Christmas* on our children's list, which are part of the 'Wow!' series, helping children creatively explore stories in the Bible.

IF THERE'S ONE THING WE ALL NEED TODAY, IT IS HOPE.

CATHY & MARK **MADAVAN**

UP AND ALIVE

LIVING THE LIFE WE ARE MADE FOR
EXPLORING THEMES IN EPHESIANS

THE OFFICIAL THEME BOOK FOR
SPRING HARVEST 2024

9780281090426 | PAPERBACK & EBOOK | 144 PAGES

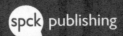

spck publishing